Heart to Heart

Premarriage Questions

Getting to "Really Know" Your Life-Mate-to-Be

BOBB AND CHERYL BIEHL

Getting to "Really Know" Your Life-Mate-to-Be

Printed in the United States of America

Design: Steven Boyd

4262-71
0-8054-6271-6

Dewey Decimal Classification: 306.81
Subject Heading: MARRIAGE
Library of Congress Card Catalog Number: 95-45310

Library of Congress Cataloging-in-Publication Data
Biehl, Bobb.
   Premarriage questions: getting to "really know" your
lifemate-to-be/ Bobb and Cheryl Biehl
     p.   cm. —(Heart to heart series)
     ISBN 0-8054-6271-6 (pbk.)
     1. Marriage—United States—Miscellanea. 2. Marriage
counseling—United States—Miscellanea. I. Biehl, Cheryl.
II. Title. III. Series.

HQ734.B62293 1996
306.81—dc20

95-45310
CIP

01 02 03 04 05 06 07 8 7 6 5 4 3 2

Contents

Introduction: A Note from the Authors vi

Part One: Before You Begin

1. An Important Decision 3
2. The Red / Yellow / Green System 5
3. Getting Started 9

Part Two: Premarriage Questions
in the Seven Areas of Life

4. Financial 13
5. Marriage and Family 17
6. Personal Growth 24
7. Physical 26
8. Professional 29
9. Social 34
10. Spiritual 38

Part Three: Taking Action

11. How to Turn a Red Light to Green 43
12. Ten Ways to Keep Your Marriage
    Healthy and Happy 45

Conclusion 49
Appendix: Additional Resources 51

✧

A Note from the Authors

Congratulations and best wishes! If you are reading this book, you are most likely engaged or just about to be engaged. Helping you have a healthy, happy, lifelong marriage is what this book is all about.

Over our thirty-plus years of marriage, we have talked with many engaged couples. Most were so excited about their upcoming marriage they could talk of little else. Many had a daily countdown running and knew precisely the number of months, weeks, days, hours, and minutes before the "I do" hour. With rare exception, questions about where they were going on their honeymoon brought smiles betraying visions of lovemaking in honeymoon suites, on deserted tropical beaches, and eventually in the apartment or little house to which they would return and set up housekeeping.

At the same time, when we would start talking to these soon-to-be-weds individually there usually would be confidential confessions of concern, expressed in the form of questions.

◇ "Is this the right time to be getting married?"
◇ "Am I really ready for marriage?"

✧ "How do I know this is *the* person God has for me?"

✧ "Am I really in love or am I just in love with the *idea* of being in love?"

✧ "How can I make sure our marriage will not end in divorce like my parents' marriage did?"

✧ "Have I asked the right questions to know how this person really thinks about the key issues in life?"

✧ "How can I know what this person will be like after we are married?"

✧ "Am I really ready to make this kind of a commitment?"

✧ "If this person really knew me as well as I know me, would they still want to marry me?"

Premarriage jitters are common. So, how do you go about settling these prenuptial jitters?

The best way of turning these anxieties into answers is by asking each other enough questions to make sure you are actually marrying the person you think you are marrying. Ask enough of the right questions and you begin to see what is in the person's heart. You see beyond the charming smile, the sexy body. You see what life will be like beyond the vow of "Till death do us part."

Most of the couples who have answered the questions in this book find the answers reassuring. "I have never been so sure that I am making the right decision, and the more I listen to this person the more certain I am that we are right for each other" is a common response. Occasionally, there is a couple whose experience is "The more I listened to her/his answers the more I knew in my heart that I did not want to spend the rest of my life married to a person who looked at life like she/he did."

Occasionally, someone confides to us, "I know this is not the person for me . . . I feel sick . . . I know I shouldn't go through with this marriage. I just don't know how to get out of it!" If this is you, use this book as your way out of the engagement. Find a question which lets you say, "As we read this book it became obvious that our marriage would never work long-term."

Blame your break up on this book. Blame it on the weather. Blame it on something, but if you know this marriage is not right . . . *do not get married!*

If this book can give you a new perspective on your relationship and help prevent the devastating effects of divorce on your life five or twenty years in the future, we will feel every hour we have invested in the book's preparation was worth a thousand times the effort.

It is our hope and prayer that you will have wisdom, patience, and understanding as you ask and answer these fun, profoundly simple, relationship-defining questions!

Bobb and Cheryl Biehl

✧

PART ONE

Before You Begin

The questions in this book are designed to help you in the process of seeing your fiancé so clearly that you make a wise decision in the choice of your lifemate.

Chapter 1
<hr/>

An Important Decision

Y ou are about to make one of life's three critical decisions.

1. Life Destiny

The single most important decision any man or woman ever makes is the decision which will reveal the determination of his or her eternal destiny. That decision is to believe and trust in Jesus Christ as Lord and Savior, to trust in self, or to trust in some other philosophy.

2. Lifemate

The second most critical decision a person makes in an entire lifetime is with whom (if anyone) he or she will become a life partner, committed to live and to grow old together in marriage. Many lives are lived in happiness and many others are lived in misery based on the wisdom of this single decision.

3. Lifework

The third most critical decision we face in life is of our career and lifework, in view of eternity ahead of us and the life partner beside us. In one sense, all of the other decisions and choices in life can be seen as reflections of these three critical decision points.

To help you get to know your fiancé at an even deeper level, we have created more than 200 fun, premarriage questions that can clarify, deepen, and strengthen your relationship. These questions cover most of the major problem areas you are likely to face as a couple.

In creating these questions we have remembered our counseling sessions with couples soon to be married, happily married, and unhappily married. We have recalled discussions in our own marriage. We remembered happy times, sad times, explosive times, loving times, and resolution times. Then, we created questions we wish someone had suggested we ask each other before *we* got married.

✧

Chapter 2

The Red / Yellow / Green System— Finding "Land Mines" before They Explode

The more you know about how your fiancé thinks and feels about a wide variety of issues and the more discussions you have *before* you get married, the fewer surprises you will encounter after you get married. After honestly discussing the questions in this book, there will be far fewer marriage-threatening surprises after the minister proudly says, "May I present Mr. and Mrs. ———."

These questions uncover differing assumptions that might otherwise have become invisible, emotional "land mines" which explode unexpectedly and cause major damage to a relationship. These questions provide a "shovel" to dig out the hidden mines before you step on them. The best time to decide whether you will live the rest of your life together is *before* the "I do," not after!

It is hard but far easier to break a dating relationship than an engagement. It is far easier to break an engagement than a marriage after the vows have been spoken and children have been conceived or born.

We do not wish to put unnecessary stress on a relationship, but rather to simply bring to light those areas in which there is existing agreement or disagreement.

This then gives you opportunity to fully enjoy your agreements and to fully explore your disagreements, before your final "In sickness and in health."

As you discuss the questions in this book, you may find only three or four that are potentially relationship-threatening disagreements. Work through these potentially explosive areas during the "deeply in love" part of your relationship.

Suppose, however, you don't discuss these issues until *after* you are married, possibly have children, and increased financial obligations. If a problem arises and one of these areas of disagreement must be faced under pressure, it creates a situation in which a marriage can blow apart and end in divorce. The devastation of divorce is what these questions are designed to prevent.

Red / Yellow / Green

A great way to communicate your agreement, or lack of agreement, on each question is the "red/yellow/green light" technique. After you have discussed a question, mark the question with a pencil in the margin using a R (red, total disagreement), Y (yellow, different conclusions or misunderstanding), or G (green, total agreement).

When you finish the book, expect to have many greens in each of the seven sections, a few yellows, and hopefully very few reds. Once a question is green, you may want to use a green marking pen or pencil to highlight those questions so that you can see at a glance how much you already agree. It's satisfying and reassuring!

Some of the questions do not require that you agree on an "answer"; you are just sharing personal experiences with each other. In that case, just mark it green when you have finished your discussion.

Go back to the yellow questions and discuss them until they turn green or red. Of the questions you mark red, there may be only two or three that actually represent "divorce potential" kinds of conflict. See chapter 11 for help in processing these questions.

Talk It Out / Write It Out

One of the advantages of these questions is that you can simply talk them out. Depending on your personal preferences, you may even want to tape record some of your answers to listen to yourselves in twenty years. This will provide great memories for you, and it may be valuable for your sons and daughters to hear the thoughts and feelings of your early married life.

If you are separated for a period of time because of career or school, you may want to write out your answers to preselected questions and send them to each other. In fact, this is a fun way to answer these questions even if you're not apart.

Although it might sound like a lot of work, writing your thoughts and feelings has many advantages:

⋄ Writing gives you time to reflect on the questions and think more about your answers.

⋄ You have a chance to present your answer in totality, without the risk of being interrupted.

⋄ Some people find it easier to write something very personal than actually say it out loud.

Whichever way you choose to discuss these questions, we hope you thoroughly enjoy the process, and that the experience helps you both communicate your thoughts, feelings, dreams, and concerns clearly to one another.

Top Ten Simple Ways to Predict a Problem Marriage

1. Getting married to spite someone else

2. Getting married without listening to close friends who are warning you of obvious problems

3. Getting married to someone of a different faith

4. Getting married with concerns and questions you are afraid to ask your fiancé

5. Getting married with things you are hiding from your fiancé that you plan to disclose once the "knot has been tied"

6. Getting married on the rebound—within months of a painful breakup

7. Getting married because you just want to get out of your parents' house

8. Getting married without dating at least twelve months

9. Getting married based primarily on a relationship of correspondence

10. Getting married because of a fear of never having another chance

These ten warning signs are not guaranteed to end in divorce. Some marriages make it in spite of built-in problems. But these are common situations which create major problems and pressures on a marriage and often end in divorce.

If you are in one of the top ten predictable problem marriage situations, it is doubly important that you take this book seriously.

✧

Chapter 3

Getting Started

There are different ways you can approach this book. Here are a few ideas:

- ✧ Start with the first category (financial) and proceed down the questions one by one until you have answered them all. Then go to the next category and do the same. Don't forget to mark each question red, yellow, or green.

- ✧ Decide together on one of the seven areas that particularly interests you at the moment (you do not have to start with financial). Start with the first question and work your way down, marking each one red, yellow, or green. There is plenty of space so you can make notes in the book about your thoughts.

- ✧ Answer three questions (or however many you decide) in one category. When those questions have been marked red, yellow, or green, then go to the next chapter and do three questions from that category. After you have answered three from each category, go back and answer three more from each category, and so on.

However you do it, we strongly suggest in each category of life that you follow the questions in order. By doing so, you eliminate the frustration of trying to find the "perfect" next question.

If you come to a question that does not apply to your relationship, just skip it and move on. Or, if a question seems too sensitive to discuss, mark it red and come back to it later.

As you answer each of the questions, you will undoubtedly think of additional questions. Write them down in the margin before you forget them.

✧

PART TWO

Premarriage Questions

The questions in this book are divided among seven basic areas of life:

Financial
Marriage and Family
Personal Growth
Physical
Professional
Social
Spiritual

❖

These seven categories have been listed alphabetically, but this is not to imply that the first on the list (financial) is more important than the last (spiritual). Note that God is not limited to the spiritual category. God is the God of families, commerce, hearts, minds, bodies, businesses, and societies, as well as the Lord of His church. So feel free to bring up the spiritual element in the discussion of any of the other categories.

✧

Chapter 4

Financial

There are few areas of married life which cause more yelling, pouting, and throwing of things than the financial area. One of the most frequent reasons given for divorce today is financial struggles and disagreements. To the extent that you are making different financial assumptions, it is likely that you will go through your marriage with some severe strains in this area. Discussing your financial assumptions will help reduce the amount of frustration, pressure, and tension you experience in this area.

Make doubly sure your assumptions are compatible in this area today, and you will be half as likely to divorce because of financial tensions tomorrow!

1. Do you see both of us working after marriage? If so, for how long?

2. How much income would you like us to make (together) during our first year of marriage?

3. In today's economy, how expensive a house do you want to live in? In five years? Ten years? Twenty years?

4. What do you think about credit cards? How many do you have now? What is the balance on each? Which cards should we have (if any) after marriage?

5. Do you see yourself as "good with keeping books" or "bad with keeping books"?

6. Will our income after marriage support the standard of living you've become accustomed to? If not, what adjustments do we need to make?

7. What are your feelings about a monthly budget?

8. What kind of car would you like to drive after we get married? In five years? Ten years? Twenty years?

9. How much do you now spend per month on clothing? How much should we spend on clothing during our first year of marriage? How much would you like to spend a year in five years? Ten years?

10. What are your total financial obligations right now? (In some situations this is a critical question.)

11. Who will write the checks to pay monthly bills?

12. Who will balance the monthly bank statement?

13. What are your feelings about joint versus separate checking accounts?

14. How would you describe yourself as a money manager?

15. For the first year of our marriage, do you want to live in a house, apartment, mobile home, condominium, or tent? Why?

16. How much money should we spend on furniture the first year? Why? Cash or credit card? What are your feelings about buying good used furniture? What furniture style do you prefer?

17. What are your feelings about a will? When do you think we should have one made? Why?

18. Do you think children should be paid for jobs around the house? Why? How much?

19. Do you think children should be given an allowance? If so, how much at ages five, ten, fifteen, twenty-one? If not, why not?

20. How much should we spend a year on luxury items such as jewelry, furs, athletic equipment, trips, etc.?

21. What percentage should we tip a server who does an outstanding job? An average job? A poor job?

22. How much should you have to pay to have your hair cut? Styled? What is a suitable tip for these services?

23. If we inherited a million dollars, what would you want to do with it?

24. What percentage of our income should we give to the place of worship we attend? Why?

25. What percentage of our income should we give to charitable organizations?

26. How much life insurance should we have? Health insurance? What company? Why?

27. Do you want to invest some of our money? How? When?

28. How do you feel about borrowing money from our parents or relatives?

29. How do you feel about loaning money to our parents or relatives?

30. Imagine that a friend of ours borrows money from us and doesn't repay it. How would you feel? What would you do?

31. How much should we spend on a getaway weekend?

32. How would you have the most amount of fun if we only had five dollars to spend some evening?

33. How much should we spend on:

   ✧ Birthdays: each other's, parents, children, friends, others (you name)
   ✧ Anniversaries: our own, parents, friends, relatives
   ✧ Other special days: Mother's Day, Father's Day, Valentine's Day
   ✧ Christmas: each other's gift, parents, children, other relatives, coworkers, friends, decorations?

34. Who should do the gift buying for birthdays? Anniversaries? Christmas? Other special days? If it's usually the same person, how can the other one help?

35. How do you feel about declaring bankruptcy?

36. What should be the dollar limit on purchases made without the other's knowledge? Why?

37. Prioritize the following typical household items as to their importance to you.

__Athletic equipment	__Compact disc player
__Color TV	__Dining room furniture
__Dishwasher	__Food dehydrator
__Food processor	__Freezer
__Hobby items	__Living room furniture
__Bedroom furniture	__Microwave
__Piano	__Stereo system
__VCR	__Video camera
__Washer/dryer	__Other:_____

✧

Chapter 5

Marriage and Family

With the lifemate decision, you are not only marrying a person of the opposite sex, you are determining:

- ❖ your future mother-in-law;
- ❖ your future father-in-law;
- ❖ your children's grandparents;
- ❖ your children's other parent;
- ❖ your future nieces and nephews, and all of the rest of your in-laws;
- ❖ where you, and your children, will likely spend Thanksgiving, Christmas, and birthdays for the next fifty plus years.

The success or failure of your marriage impacts a lot of people. Communicate honestly and clearly on these issues. Your extended family for generations to come will be influenced by your discussions and your decisions.

1. How often do you feel it is important to go out to dinner rather than cook at home?

2. Describe your idea of an ideal week of evenings? What would you like to do Monday night? Tuesday, etc.?

3. How do you want to celebrate our wedding anniversary each year (in general)?

4. Is there something fun or special you've always wanted us to do, but we haven't yet had the money or taken the time?

5. What do you picture us doing on our first vacation?

6. Ideally, how many children would you want to have? Do you have any preferences about how many boys? Girls? How many years between them?

7. How do you think you would respond if we had a severely disabled child?

8. What are your thoughts and feelings about abortion?

9. What would you do if one of our children wanted to marry someone of another race or ethnic group?

10. How do you feel about birth control? If you think we should use something, what method do you see as the best one for us?

11. How do you think you would feel if we were not able to have children? In that case, how do you feel about adoption?

12. What three things do you expect to be most rewarding about parenting? The three most frustrating?

13. What are the five things you definitely want me to do for and with our children?

14. What do you see as your role as a parent with our children? My role?

15. What would be the five most strictly enforced rules of our house for child discipline?

16. What five to ten foundational biblical truths do you think should be stressed in the raising of children?

17. How often should we as parents get away from babies in their first year. How often when the children are older?

18. How do you feel about nursery schools? About day-care centers? What are the advantages? Disadvantages?

19. If it's a holiday and you want a new outfit, and the baby also needs new clothing, and you can only afford one, who would get the new outfit and why?

20. How much would you guess it costs to care for a baby per month in the first year? (You may want to double-check with a couple who has a new baby, to see if your guesses are in the "ball park.")

21. What style of discipline would you use with a toddler? Elementary-age child? Junior higher? High schooler? College-age?

22. How do you feel about spanking a child? Under what conditions? With what instrument?

23. What do you think about having our elementary-age children in Sunday School or church? Junior highers? High schoolers?

24. Do you think elementary-age children should be in a public or private school? What about home schooling? What about older children? Why?

25. At what age should a son begin to date? When should a daughter begin to date? What should be our house rules for curfew?

26. How much of a child's college education should be paid by the parents? Under what conditions?

27. How much freedom and responsibility should children be given at age five? Ten? Fifteen?

28. How do you feel about male or female surgery to avoid having more children? At what number of children, or under what circumstances, would you consider it necessary to take precautions not to have more children?

29. Are there areas in which we may be a bad example to our children? What can we do about this?

30. What does the phrase "Till death do us part" mean to you?

31. Do you see divorce as an option in any circumstances? If so, in what circumstances?

32. If there has been divorce in your immediate family, what preventive steps can we take to avoid similar disruptive patterns in our relationship?

33. What would you do if I became totally incapacitated and could never have sex or children?

34. What would be your response if I developed cancer or broke my back and was partially paralyzed?

35. What if our marriage doesn't turn out to be quite as much fun as you expected it to be?

36. What if my job required me to be away from home a week or two at a time? Do you feel you could handle being alone that much without being tempted to "run around"? Do you feel I could handle being alone?

37. When we disagree with one another, how should we settle it?

38. What do you think about marital counseling? Why? What are the advantages? Done by whom?

39. What are your five most positive expectations about our married life together?

40. What are your five greatest concerns or lingering questions about our married life together?

41. How much television do you watch each day? Mostly what kind of programs do you watch? How do you feel about having the television turned on for most of the day?

42. What's involved in "romance" for you? How important to you are those elements in our marriage?

43 How often do you think a person should take a shower/bath? Brush teeth? Change the bathroom towels? Vacuum and dust? Wash out the tub?

44. What kind of music do you like? Dislike?

45. What are three of your happiest memories of our life together so far? Why?

46. What couple, whom you know personally, has the most ideal marriage? Why do you think it is so ideal? Who could we talk to who would help us understand and deal with our concerns before we actually marry?

47. Deep down, how does your mother feel about our relationship? Your father? Brothers and sisters?

48. What words would you use to describe your parents' marriage and relationship? Why? Your grandparent's marriage?

49. What are the three things you admire most about each of your parents as a marriage partner?

50. What are the three things you admire most about each of your parents as people?

51. What changes would you want to make from your childhood in relation to raising our own family?

52. If one of our parents became widowed or seriously ill, what would you think should be our responsibility to him/her?

53. Do you foresee any of our relatives interfering in our marriage? Who? How? What would we do if that happened?

54. How do you feel about an unmade bed in the middle of the day?

55. Who do you think is responsible to do the following work around the home?

Car repairs	Christmas tree
Cooking	Dishes
Fixing things	Grocery shopping
House cleaning	Insurance
Ironing clothes	Making the bed
Washing clothes	Yard work
Other _____	

56. What are your three favorite thoughts about making love after we're married?

57. What are five assumptions you have about how I will make love?

58. What are your taboos or things you do not want to do at all in lovemaking?

59. From your perspective, what are the most important things to be aware of when making love?

60. Are there any "skeletons" of any kind in your past? Bankruptcy, abortion, divorce, arrest, prison time, etc.? (Avoid surprises after saying "I do." Talk about these things before the final commitment, not on your honeymoon!)

61. Are you a night person or a morning person? How would you suggest we adjust?

62. What would be the advantages of waiting one more year before getting married? What would be the disadvantages?

63. How long do you think we should be married before having children?

✧

Chapter 6

Personal Growth

Remember back ten years. Talk about what life was like for each of you then. Could you possibly have imagined where you would be today? It would have been just as easy for you to imagine today ten years ago as it would be to imagine ten years from now—today!

Point: You will both continue to grow rapidly, but how do you each want to grow, and in what direction? Where do you each feel held back?

1. A year from today, in what three to five areas of your life would you most like to be stronger than you are now?

2. In what three areas would you most like to see me grow in the next year? Why?

3. What do you feel are the three key things keeping you from reaching your full potential today?

4. If you could become the "world expert" in any one area or subject, what would it be?

5. What moral/social/political issues would you like to know more about? Why?

6. What five books would you most like to read? Why?

7. Name five of your all-time favorite books. What did you like about them? Would you like me to read them?

8. If you could sit and chat with any person in the world, with whom would you talk? What three questions would you ask that person? Why?

9. What do you consider your three greatest strengths to be maximized in the future? What is your single greatest strength?

10. If we could improve only one aspect of the way we relate to each other, what would that be? Why?

11. What keeps you from getting excited about being promoted at work or taking on more responsibility?

12. What negative comment did someone make about you years ago which is still holding back your confidence? How can I help you overcome that blockage in your life?

13. In what three areas of your life do you think you have grown most in the last several years?

14. What three people have had the greatest impact in your life? Why?

15. Who was your best friend in grade school? Junior high? High school? College? How did each contribute to your personal growth at that time of your life?

✧

Chapter 7

Physical

One basic reality in life is: *We all change physically as we grow older.*

What are your thoughts about your own physical appearance and that of your life partner? How do you actually *feel* about your weight, your sex appeal, and your overall image?

✧

1. How do you feel about an exercise program for you and me? What kind? How often?

2. What kind of physical exercise would you most like to do together? Separately?

3. What five things do you like best about my physical appearance?

4. What three suggestions would you like to make about how I can improve my physical appearance?

5. How do you feel about taking vitamins and nutritional supplements? How much per month should be spent on them?

6. Would you prefer to go to a medical doctor or a nutritionist?

7. How do you feel about going to chiropractors?

8. How do you feel about the food we eat? What changes would you make? Are you willing to help make changes (shopping, cooking, studying, etc.)?

9. Based on your family's medical history, do you have any anxieties about your health either now or in the future? How would you feel if I developed one of these conditions?

10. How do you feel about me being overweight? How do you feel about you being overweight? How many pounds do you think is overweight?

11. How do you feel about baldness? Wrinkles? Gray hair?

12. Do you have any desire to belong to a recreational club, such as YMCA, or to a country club? Why?

13. Do you have a favorite recreational activity? How often do you participate in it now? Does it require continual updating of equipment? How much do you spend in a year on that activity?

14. How do you feel about getting older? Thirty? Forty? Fifty? Sixty? Seventy?

15. Specifically, what do you plan to do in order to avoid the potential of having an affair?

16. How do you prefer I wear my hair? How do you feel about beards, mustaches, sideburns? How many buttons should I leave open on a shirt or blouse?

17. What is your favorite outfit/clothing, and why do you enjoy it?

18. What five nationally known personalities do you most identify with and would most like to be like?

19. Who are five national and visible personalities you find most attractive sexually, and what is it about them that you find attractive? How will you deal with the difference between what you find attractive in others of the opposite sex and what I am not?

20. What physical dimensions "turn you off" sexually? What "turns you on" sexually?

21. How do you feel about alcoholic beverages? Cigarettes? Pipes or cigars? Mind-altering drugs?

22. What are your feelings about pornographic magazines, movies, etc.? Explain.

23. How do you feel about the differences in our natural energy level?

24. How much fresh air do you like when sleeping? If you use an electric blanket, where do you set the temperature—closer to 1 or 10?

✧

Chapter 8

Professional

As a person matures he/she moves through phases like.
"I got the job!"
"I think I'll choose this field as my profession."
"My career is progressing well . . . or in a slump."
"What will my lifework be?"
As each of you progresses in age and professional experience, it is critical that you are both making the same basic assumptions concerning work!

✧

1. How do you feel about my work? What do you like best about it? Is there anything about my work that frustrates or worries you?

2. What type of work do you think I would do best?

3. What would you consider my top three alternative careers? Why do you think these would be good things for me to pursue?

4. To what professional or work-related associations or groups should you, or I, or we belong? Why?

5. What company, organization, or firm would you most like to work with if you had your choice? Why?

6. How would you feel about my working with the _____ company?

7. What do you consider the five most important factors in bringing you happiness or satisfaction in your work? How many of those factors are present in your work now?

8. What work-related or professional goals will you have to reach to feel really successful in life?

9. What brings you the most satisfaction in your job or career? In the relationships at work?

10. What kind of work brings you personal fulfillment?

11. How important to you is the feeling that you are making a significant difference in your work?

12. How would you describe the difference between having a job, a profession, a career, and a lifework?

13. How important is it to you to have fun on your job?

14. How important to you is being a member of the team at work? Of being accepted by that team?

15. What will you have to learn, do, or become before you are ready for the next promotion at work?

16. How important is *security* in any career you would choose? Why?

17. How do you feel about a job or career for me that would include travel? How much travel would be acceptable to you? How much would you find unacceptable?

18. How important to you is our parents' acceptance of what I do as a profession? Our children's acceptance?

19. Would you rather work with your hands, your head, or your back?

20. If you could have anyone's job in the world, whose job would you have and why?

21. What do you definitely *not* want in your lifework?

22. How would you feel about us working together as a two-person team at some time in the future? If you would feel good about that, what would you see us doing together?

23. In your heart of hearts, how do you feel about a wife having a separate career from her husband, where she may need as much support to keep going in her profession as the husband would in his?

24. How would you feel about me making more (or less) money than you, if that should happen?

25. What is it in a job, profession, or career that you would definitely *not* want me to be part of in the future?

26. If I had all the time, energy, and money I needed and could have any position or work, what position or work would you ideally like me to have? Why?

27. If my work responsibilities required me to move to another location, in what parts of the country/world would you feel comfortable living? Where would you definitely *not* want to live? Why?

28. If my work required a move and yours did not, how would we decide what to do?

29. Under what circumstances do you feel a wife should (should not) work outside the home?

30. How would you feel about me working a swing shift? A night shift?

31. How would you feel about me working two jobs?

32. How do you think your father feels (felt) about his work? How do you feel about his work?

33. While you were growing up, did your mother work outside the home? Either way, how did you feel about it? Why?

34. If you were ever fired from a job in which you were happy, how would you want me to relate to you when you came home from work?

35. What is the highest position you can imagine me holding at some time in the future?

36. How would you feel about me if I became a: Full-time Christian minister? Corporate executive? Factory worker? Farmer? Lawyer? Medical professional (doctor, nurse, etc.)? Missionary? Movie star? Psychologist? Police officer? Politician? Rock singer? Salesperson? Self-employed? Truck driver?

37. If the career I chose required me to spend three to ten years of preparation before I could become successful, how would you feel about waiting that long?

38. How would you feel about me if, after five years of working hard in some business or profession, I failed at that work?

39. How would you feel about starting a business from scratch where there was a major risk to the money we invested from our savings?

40. Would you prefer that I be on a lower fixed salary or a higher potential commission with no guaranteed income? Why?

41. If I decided to go back to school for further education, how would you feel about that decision? Why? What would be the advantages? Disadvantages?

42. If you could start a business with anyone, what three people would you choose to be partners? Why?

43. If we started a business together, what would you want to do in that business?

44. Would you hesitate to start a business of our own? Why?

❖

Chapter 9

Social

Friendships are invaluable! Social times are priceless! However, are we making the same assumptions about our social life? Do we really enjoy the same people, the same parties, or entertaining in the same way?

❖

1. How would you guess our social relationships with each of our current friends will change when we get married?

2. One year after we're married, what differences would you anticipate in our social life? After five years? After twenty years?

3. How do you feel about me going "out with the guys" (or gals, friends of the same gender)? How often?

4. What do you think my future relationship should be with friends of the opposite sex (friendships I had prior to marriage)? (Name each one specifically, especially past romantic relationships, and discuss each of your assumptions about those relationships.)

5. How do you feel about parties? What kind do you most enjoy? Least enjoy? Want to avoid at all costs?

6. What is the best party you've ever attended? Why did you enjoy it?

7. How confident are you socially, on a scale of one to ten (where one is insecure and ten is extremely confident)? How does your confidence at a party change when we are there together, as compared to your being there alone?

8. Who are your five closest friends? Why do you enjoy them? How do you think I feel about them? Who are five people you used to have as friends but have drifted from? Why did those friendships drift, and how does it make you feel when you reflect on them?

9. When going out, what do you enjoy doing most with another couple or small group of people?

10. How do you feel about having friends "pop in"? Your relatives? My relatives?

11. How do you feel about us "popping in" on friends? Your relatives? My relatives?

12. How do you feel about having out-of-town friends stay overnight with us? Out-of-town relatives?

13. How do you feel about staying with friends when we travel (as opposed to staying in hotels)?

14. If we were to take a trip with another couple within five hundred miles of home, what would you want to do? How long would you want to stay? Where would you want to go? With whom?

15. How many nights a month would you be open to guests staying in our home?

16. What qualities do your friends have in common? What do you look for in a friend?

17. What do you feel you give to a friendship or to a social relationship?

18. How would you improve on either one of our social lives?

19. What are the social situations in which you feel least comfortable and why?

20. What are the social situations in which you feel most confident and why?

21. What do you enjoy most doing on an evening out? Why?

22. What elements of a social event make you frustrated? Disapppointed? Angry? Uncomfortable?

23. If you could go to any "high society" event in the world, which would you most enjoy? Why?

24. If you could go back in history, what social event would you enjoy most attending? Why?

25. If we were given $2,000 to go somewhere just for fun, where would you want to go? Why?

26. If we had $200 to spend on an evening out, how would you want to spend it?

27. If we had only $20 to do something "wild and crazy" together, what would you want to do?

28. What kind of parties do you find most enjoyable (theme parties, costume parties, Valentine parties, Christmas parties, etc.)? Why?

29. If we were to go to dinner on three separate evenings with three different married couples, what three couples would you most enjoy going to dinner with?

30. If we were to go to a foreign country with a couple, what country would you choose? With whom? Why?

31. How many evenings a week (or a month) would you enjoy socializing with friends as a married couple? Why?

32. On a Friday or Saturday night, if the choice was between staying home and reading, or going out to a movie or party, which would you honestly prefer?

33. Where would you like to meet new friends in the future? (church, work, family, etc.)?

34. How do you feel about your parents' social life? How do you feel about my parents' social life?

✧

Chapter 10

Spiritual

Politics and religion are two American taboos of polite conversation. In marriage, however, these topics are "must discussions!" The Bible warns about being "unequally yoked," or being of different faiths, as a foundation for your marriage.

Take your time and discuss each of these questions as openly as possible. Ten years from now, you will be pleased that you did!

1. When you lean back in your chair and imagine heaven, what do you see?

2. How do you feel about the church in general?

3. How often do you want to attend church after we are married?

4. Is the church you (we) attend teaching the truths of the Bible?

5. What do you enjoy doing or being involved with in a church?

6. What type of worship service do you prefer?

7. How often do you read the Bible? How often would you like us to read the Bible together? Why?

8. What does prayer mean to you?

9. How do you feel about our having a devotional time together? Why?

10. How would you feel about my being a member of the clergy someday? Why?

11. What are three highlights of your spiritual life?

12. What was a low point of your spiritual life?

13. To you, what are some important, nonnegotiable, biblical issues, principles, or doctrines? Why?

14. If you could ask God any three questions on any topic, what would you ask? Why?

15. What do you believe the Bible says about marriage and divorce?

16. How do you feel about and think about Jesus?

17. In what area of your spiritual life do you feel the greatest need for personal growth?

18. From your perspective, what are three keys to a strong spiritual life?

19. If I felt led of God to move to Africa and work with some tribal group, what would be your reaction?

20. What are your beliefs about hell? About heaven? Why?

21. How confident are you right now of your salvation?

22. Is there a specific church or denomination that is important to you? Why? Is there a specific church or denomination you would not want to be involved with? Why?

23. What do you believe is God's standard regarding sexual relationships within marriage? Sexual relationships outside of marriage?

24. When making a major decision, how do you determine God's will?

25. From a biblical perspective, what do you believe to be the husband's responsibility to his wife? To his children? To the spiritual welfare of his wife and children? In each area, what are examples of practical ways you see this responsibility being carried out in our marriage?

26. From a biblical perspective, what do you believe to be the wife's responsibility to her husband? To her children? To the spiritual welfare of her husband and children? In each area, what are examples of practical ways you see this responsibility being carried out in our marriage?

27. How strong are (were) your parents' spiritual convictions?

28. Do you tithe (give 10 percent of your income) regularly to your church? Do you plan to continue tithing after marriage? Do you think a tithe is based on net or gross income? Do you think that all of the tithe must go to the local church?

✧

Taking Action

*If you disagree on a question,
the first thing you ask is:
"Is this an important issue to me? To us?"*

*If your difference of opinion is on something
that both of you consider insignificant,
then you don't need to read any further.
Simply go to the next question and enjoy
discovering more about each other.*

✧

Chapter 11

How to Turn
a Red Light to Green

If the red light is an issue of significance to *either one* of you, there is more than one conflict-resolution skill or approach available. We will not list all of them for you. Our objective is to give you a few ideas on how to approach the conflict. They may or may not work for every yellow or red issue, but you should be able to make headway toward a green.

If these ideas do not work, we suggest that the two of you seek a wise friend or a qualified minister or counselor. Tell that person what you have discussed about the issue.

Never be concerned or embarrassed about seeking qualified help. Your marriage is a precious asset and should be nurtured and cared for with wisdom. Marriage often takes more wisdom than any two people alone can provide.

Unfortunately, many times, either the husband or wife won't even consider talking to a counselor until one announces he or she is leaving the relationship. Then the reluctant one is willing to talk, but in many cases, it is too little, too late.

Ideas to Consider

1. Express your thoughts and feelings openly yet sensitively. You cannot resolve a difference if you choose to be passive or silent.

2. Commit to the resolution of the disagreement and work on it. You cannot resolve a difference if one partner chooses to be less than 100 percent involved in making it work.

3. Realize the importance of the resolution of serious conflict. You can certainly live together without red lights resolved, but your relationship will be weakened and possibly vulnerable to problems.

These questions have been designed to help you make a wise decision. We want what is best for both of you. It is our prayer that these questions helped you see that your potential mate will be your lifelong friend and spouse. We feel honored that you let us be a part of your decision-making process.

Chapter 12

Ten Ways to Keep Your Marriage Healthy and Happy

The following ten thoughts will help keep you focused on developing a healthy, happy marriage.

✧

1. Commit "till death do us part"—you have made a vow to God and to another much-loved human being.

✧ Dream together—look forward to things.

✧ Be loyal to your mate at all costs.

✧ Care more about what your mate thinks of you than what your friends do.

2. Develop a common spiritual commitment.

✧ Pray for your mate regularly.

✧ Pray together regularly.

✧ Worship together.

3. Want what is best for your lifemate.

✧ Focus on what's right with your mate, not what's wrong with him/her.

✧ Work as a team—rely on each other's strength.

✧ Serve your mate.

4. Spend time with model couples who have been happily married ten to twenty years longer than you.

✧ Develop a relationship with a personal mentor to help you when times are tough, giving you wise counsel.

✧ Spend time with peer couples that have healthy, happy marriages.

5. Understand that no marriage is perfect and no partner is perfect. Give grace to be different.

✧ No one wants to fail. Your mate is doing the best he/she can at the moment.

✧ Don't take all emotional explosions personally. Sometimes your mate just needs to let off steam!

✧ Let the relationship breathe. A couple needs time together and away. When things get tense, you may just need a few hours or days away.

6. Find time to communicate—walking on the beach, telephoning, traveling together.

✧ Communicating, traveling together.
—Listen to your mate's heart, not just to words.
—Let your mate vent emotions without feeling you have to "fix it"!

✧ Settling differences
—Don't pout; stay and talk it out.
—"Clarify" your concerns if you don't like to "confront."
—Listen carefully. Allow the other to complete his/her thoughts without you interrupting, moving off the subject, or waiting impatiently to make your point.

7. Develop common interests.

✧ Enjoy hobbies and friends.

❖ Do fun things together—concerts, plays, picnics.

❖ Travel together whenever you get a chance.

8. Get to know your mate at the deepest level possible.

❖ Study your mate—what turns her/him off and on sexually, nonverbal signals, foreplay, moods, etc.

❖ Know precisely what your mate needs from you.

9. Avoid:

❖ negative kidding—saying negative things you don't really mean that secretly hurt and do serious damage to one's confidence and one's natural love;

❖ conditional love—basing your love on actions of any kind;

❖ waiting for your mate to meet your needs before you will meet hers/his;

❖ talking negatively about your mate's parents.

10. Be romantic, not just sexy.

❖ Splurge occasionally.

❖ Do small things which communicate "Thinking only of you . . . Thought of you while I was away . . . You are the center of my universe!"

❖ Talk with a loving, caring, tender tone in your voice, not an angry, harsh, bitter tone.

Ten Affordable Ways to Rekindle Your Romance

1. Take a little time off work—walk on the beach or in a forest, prepare a picnic away from everyone and everything, alone together.

2. Say "I love you" ten ways in one day without words.

3. Share something from your heart with your mate you have never told anyone about yourself.

4. Express every positive thought/feeling you have: "You smell good, I like your hairstyle, you have great hands, your voice is like the wind" (whatever you do, do not add "like a tornado"!).

5. Make your bedroom a special romantic place: use candles, lights, lace, etc.

6. Attend weddings and funerals together. It reminds you how fortunate you are to be alive and in love!

7. Give a few flowers, a bit of poetry, or a simple "just thinking of you" gift.

8. Call in the middle of the day just to say "I love you!"

9. A simple greeting card for no reason is very romantic—especially if it contains a short, loving, handwritten expression of the true love in your heart.

10. A full body massage is always nice—and is always affordable.

We hope these ten suggestions are as helpful to you as they have been to us.

✧

Conclusion

This book is intended to maximize your marriage, not undermine it. Although some of the questions may seem threatening, look at them as an opportunity to learn more about yourself as well as your partner. As you both have a better understanding of each other, you will be able to handle the stresses that inevitably come in a marriage.

We are not for or against your getting married. We are for your marriage if it will last the rest of your life. We are against your marriage if it will not bring you a mutually satisfying relationship, possibly ending in the pain of divorce.

Choosing your life partner is, we believe, one of the three most critical decisions you will ever make. In order to make the right decision, you both must work carefully, taking the time to clarify assumptions.

Remember: It's far easier to call off an engagement today than it is to go through a divorce tomorrow.

Disagreements on basic issues—unresolved red lights—need not be engagement breakers. You may just need help sorting out assumptions, understanding motivations, and clearing up communication. Don't hesitate to seek the help of a counselor to work through these differences. After all, a lifetime commitment is at stake.

These questions are not for one-time use. You can go through most of them once a year for the rest of your life and have fresh answers and gain new insights each time.

Your marriage should be based on a relationship which is secure, lasting, and mutually beneficial. It's our prayer that these questions have helped you make a wise and lifelong decision!

Invite us to your fiftieth anniversary party!

✧

Additional Resources by Bobb and Cheryl Biehl

Asking to Win!
This booklet (part of our Pocket Confidence series) goes in your suit coat pocket, briefcase, or purse. It contains one hundred questions—ten questions to ask in each of the following situations:

1. Asking—personal questions to avoid "small talk"
2. Brainstorming—to maximize your very finest ideas
3. Career-ing—when you or a friend are considering changing careers
4. Deciding—when a risky, pressurized, costly decision needs to be made
5. Interviewing—getting behind the smile of a potential team member
6. Focusing—putting your life into focus, or refocus
7. Organizing—to maximize your time
8. Parenting—to raise healthy, balanced children
9. Planning—any organization or major project
10. Solving—questions to solve problems faster

These booklets are packaged and priced reasonably enough for you to give to adult children, colleagues, friends, proteges, spouses, staff members.

Career Change Questions / Lifework

Thirty Questions to Ask before Making Any Major Career Change

This series of thirty questions comes in handy any time you are thinking about making a career change. These questions save you hours of uncertainty.

Focusing By Asking

If it seems you just never have time as a couple to do what you most want to do, consider listening to this CD together and making some specific prioritizing decisions.

Staff Evaluation-135

Have you ever wanted a comprehensive evaluation checklist for telling your mate exactly how he or she is doing, on a 1–10 scale, in everything from bad breath to decision making?

This is it—135 dimensions in all. This is an ideal annual tool for you to use with those close to you. And, if you like, let them evaluate you. This list helps maximize communication while concentrating on the positive.

Focusing Your Life

Focusing Your Life is a simple, step-by-step process you learn to help "clear the fog" and keep you focused for the rest of your life. This great book helps you reflect on your future!

Mentoring: How to Find One and How to Become One

This booklet gives you very useful steps about forming a mentoring relationship and answers practical mentoring questions with tried and true answers. Consider finding a mentor couple to help you through some of the tight places in life.

On My Own Handbook

If you have been concerned about your high school or college student's readiness to face the "real world," this book has been written for your son or daughter.

Many adults have said that they wish their parents had taught them these principles before they started off "on their own." Parents, as well as students, benefit from these extremely fundamental leadership principles.

These principles will stay with your son or daughter for a lifetime. And they likely will pass many on to their children's children.

Heart to Heart

Premarriage Questions- Fun questions to ask before you get married, to help you have a healthy, happy, lifelong marriage.

We want you to have a perfect marriage, or as close to it as possible. This affordable paperback book helps you ask fresh, stimulating, fun, intimate, enlightening questions of your mate, to make sure your marriage has as solid a foundation as possible.

Stop Setting Goals

When a husband is a goal setter and the wife a problem solver, there are many predictable problems. When a wife is a goal setter and the husband is a problem solver, there are many predictable problems. When both husband and wife are goal setters or both problem solvers, there are many predictable problems. This book helps you determine which you are, and how (as a couple) to maximize your differences instead of being hurt by them.

The Question Book

A high percentage of marital frustration, tension, and pressure comes in the decision-making process. But when unwise decisions are made without asking the basic, probing questions, it adds to the household tension.

Ninety-nine experts give you the twenty questions they would teach their own son or daughter to ask before making an important decision in their area of expertise.

The Question Book is a life-long reference book. Written in a classic style, it will never really be "out of date." Topics are alphabetically easy to find.

Why You Do What You Do

This book is a result of more than 21,000 hours of behind-the-lines experiences with some of the finest, emotionally healthy leaders of our generation.

This model was developed to maximize "healthy" people with a few emotional "mysteries" still unanswered! It answers questions (about your spouse) like:

✧ Why does he/she have a phobic fear of failure, rejection, or insignificance?

✧ Why is he/she so "driven" to be admired, recognized, appreciated, secure, respected, or accepted?

✧ Why is he/she an enabler, leader, promoter, rescuer, controller, people-pleaser?

✧ Why is he/she a perfectionist, workaholic, or "withdrawer" from tough situations?

✧ Where is he/she most vulnerable to the temptation of an affair?

✧ Why does he/she have such a hard time relating to his /her parents?

✧ Why does he/she sometimes seem like a child?

These and other emotional mysteries can be understood and resolved in the silence of your own heart and marriage without years of therapy.

Wisdom for Men

This is a small, easy-to-read gift book for any Christian husband. It contains life principles combined with parallel Scriptures to give wise perspective on many topics.

To learn when Bobb or Cheryl will be speaking in your area, or to learn more about any of the resources listed above, contact is possible in the following ways:

WRITE:
> Bobb and Cheryl Biehl
> c/o Masterplanning Group International
> Post Office Box 952499
> Lake Mary, Florida 32795-2499

TELEPHONE:
> To contact the Biehl's office (answered "Masterplanning Group"), call 1-407-330- 2028.

> To order materials, call 1-800-443-1976.

FAX:
> 1-407-330-4134